LITTLE HOUSE OF OXYMORONS

LITTLE HOUSE OF OXYMORONS

WITH COMMENTARIES

Steven Carter

Hamilton Books
A member of
The Rowman & Littlefield Publishing Group
Lanham · Boulder · New York · Toronto · Plymouth, UK

Copyright © 2010 by
Hamilton Books
4501 Forbes Boulevard
Suite 200
Lanham, Maryland 20706
Hamilton Books Acquisitions Department (301) 459-3366

Estover Road
Plymouth PL6 7PY
United Kingdom

Library of Congress Control Number: 2010924026
ISBN: 978-0-7618-5103-5 (paperback : alk. paper)
eISBN: 978-0-7618-5104-2

For Barry Bainton

Author's Note to the Reader

*L*ittle House of Oxymorons is a work of satire designed to complement my two-volume *The New Devil's Dictionary,*[1] published in Europe in 2008 and 2009 by the Instituto Italiano di Cultura di Napoli under the auspices of UNESCO.

Certainly not all oxymorons are satirical. *The American Heritage Dictionary* (3rd edition) defines the word as a "rhetorical figure in which incongruous or contradictory terms are combined, as in *a deafening silence* and *a mournful optimist.*" Beyond this conventional classification, and in *The New Devil's Dictionary*, here I've tried to honor the satirist's injunction to hold up a mirror that reflects a little more, perhaps, than some readers would like. Oxymoronically speaking, if readers also happen to find some of the contents of *Little House* funny, I'll feel I've done.my job.

"The bower"
Swan Lake, Montana

---

1. A third volume is in progress.

Little House of Oxymorons

Above suspicion

Many, in fact, are beneath it.

❧

Acid trip

LSD got you nowhere, unless you call tripping about in your own head getting somewhere. Also remember that as a verb "trip" means "to stumble."

❧

Amateur athlete

These days, there are precious few exceptions to this oxymoron, among them NCAA Women's Softball: no agents coming out of the woodwork; no money under the table; very little attitude; no one-and-done in the college ranks, et cetera.

❧

Apartment home

Also a euphemism, "Apartment home" is a phrase which you'll find in the classifieds, and is the real estate equivalent of the car dealership's tacky "pre-owned" (used) or "transportation counselor" (salesman).

Australian culture

Don't get the Australian native and art critic Robert Hughes started on the subject of "Australian culture," especially in the western part of that continent.

Autodidact

Teacher with a dunce for a student.

Balanced news

FOX likes to boast that its news department is "fair, balanced, and objective," and that it "brings you the facts and lets you decide." The other day, Studio B with Shepard Smith featured a story about a guy sentenced to life without parole for murdering his wife. The reason he gave for shooting her three times in the head was that he didn't like his sex life.

"Wonder how he'll like it now?" was Shepard Smith's rhetorical question to the TV audience.

కింళ

BBC English

Unintelligible to everyone, particularly the British.

కింళ

Beneath contempt

See "Above suspicion."

కింళ

Better half

Ambrose Bierce prefers "bitter half."

৵৽

Big Easy

Alas, after Hurricane Katrina, New Orleans is no longer Big or Easy.

৵৽

Big shot

Little man!

৵৽

Big wheel

See "Big Shot."

৵৽

Bilingual

Inarticulate in two languages.

৵৽

Binding arbitration

The loopholes come hard upon!

৵৽

Bipartisan consensus

Nancy Pelosi's infelicitous phrase (April 2009): the hypocritical and intransigent Pelosi, whose utter disdain for Republicans is well-known.

Blame game

An expense of spirit in a waste of blame! No one accepts blame anyway, at least not according to the rules on the Hill.

Blind justice

The "white cane": an all-too-common failure on the part of many cops and even some judges to see a difference between the spirit and the letter of the law.

Blizzard State

This moniker earns its oxymoronic spurs as one nickname for *Texas*, of all places.

Blueberry

More purplish than blue and not much of a berry; bland-tasting, especially in pies.

Bon mot

Literally: "good word." Not on the Hill.

Bower of bliss

A mythical grove of trees in the Garden of Eden; blissful, that
is, until Adam and Eve happened by and did their thing.

Brain trust

Trust me: your typical Wall Street brain trust will screw things
up all over again in 2011.

Bridegroom

A most curious compound word, at loggerheads with itself.

Brief word

I'll bet the ranch that no one who says "I'd like a brief word with you" is ever, ah, true to his word in any way, shape, or form.

Broken-hearted

In Ernest Hemingway's short story "Ten Indians," the young Nick Adams learns that his Indian girlfriend has been observed (by Nick's father) thrashing about in the bushes with a boy named Frank Washburn. He goes to bed, thinking: "My heart's broken. If I feel this way, my heart must be broken." Then:

> When he awoke in the night he heard the wind in the hemlock trees outside the cottage and the waves of the lake coming in on the shore, and he went back to sleep. In the morning there was a big wind blowing and the waves were running high up on the beach and he was awake a long time before he remembered that his heart was broken.

Busman's holiday

Probably not meant to refer to garbage-men or sewer workers!

Campus housing

Anyone who's lived in the dorms on most college campuses will tell you that the term "housing" doesn't make the nut.

Carefree, Arizona

A retirement city near Phoenix where aging citizens have more cares about the present and future state of their health than you can shake a Medicare policy at.

Carthaginian peace

This Roman euphemism for Roman tyranny didn't amuse the Carthaginians.

Categorical imperative

Kant's version of the Golden Rule: categorically ignored by untold millions who, throughout the dreary history of warfare, have found it imperative to kill one another as assiduously and efficiently as inhumanly possible.

Character witness

The literal personification of blind justice.

Christian Science

Little Christianity, zero science; a well-meaning religion on the skids.

Comic Strip

In the post-*Calvin and Hobbes* era, of the scores of comic strips out there only a precious few are funny. Top three: *Doonesbury, B.C.* by the late Johnny Hart, and *Get Fuzzy*. Runner-up: the venerable *Beetle Bailey*. *Peanuts* ran out of gas forty years ago.

Community college

Half-right; the community *is* involved, sort of.

Compassionate conservative

My write-in candidate for the most egregious political slogan in recent memory.

བྷ·ஜ

Considered opinion

Opinion.

བྷ·ஜ

Conventional wisdom

True wisdom is *un*conventional, to say the least, ever and always.

བྷ·ஜ

Court seal

Sieve.

Cowboy poetry

-*Cf.* the work of Arizona's "cowboy-poet" Baxter Black.

Creeping socialism

These days, socialism "creeps" in no way, shape, or form; it gallops.[1]

---

1. Today's headline: "US Government Now Runs General Motors."

Customer service

Your call is important to us.

Deep pockets

Sometimes this phrase means the opposite—i.e., someone whose pockets are so "deep" he can never find his money.

Definitely probably

"It was definitely probably the greatest catch I ever made."
—Carl Crawford, Most Valuable Player of major league baseball's 2009 All-Star Game.

Director's cut

For some strange reason so named because it includes scenes the director wisely chose to leave on the cutting room floor.

Diverse community

The problem with the PC police is that they confuse "diverse" with "unified"; not at all the same thing, gentlemen and ladies.

DMZ

In Vietnam, a quasi-mythical "zone" that was in no way, shape, or form de-militarized.

Doctor of Education

D.e(a)D.

༠‿༠

Domestic bliss

Enough said.

༠‿༠

Doublethink

Double-zero thinking; in this case "thinking" should be in scare quotes.

༠‿༠

Drug war

The problem with the drug war is that it really isn't meant to be a war against drugs at all; rather, it's "waged" against the underclass. Druggies don't make revolutions.

Duck and cover

Remember those grainy black-and-white newsreels of schoolkids in the fifties kneeling next to their desks, behinds in the air, trying to "cover" against a possible nuclear blast? All "duck and cover" meant was that you were going to get it ass-first instead of face-first.

Easy Street

The next one over!

Efficiency expert

A facilitator, or: one who makes things worse.

❧❧

Elephant bird

Turkey.

❧❧

Ethnic cleansing

A most obscene oxymoron and—needless to add—the most pernicious of euphemisms.

❧❧

Even keel

"When things go smoothly": which they never do.

Ex nihilo

The ultimate Creation Myth.

Exit strategy

Quagmire.

Extreme sports

Extremely stupid stunts: certainly not sports.

❧❦

Fail safe

A precarious, very scary nuclear war strategy; it only needs to fail once.

❧❦

Family hour

When parents are downstairs watching TV and the kids are in their rooms, texting and playing video games.

❧❦

Fast food

Of course it's fast. On the other hand, traveling through Ely, Nevada, we reluctantly stopped at a McDonalds, the only game in town. Half-way through her Big Mac, my wife, measured about most things, said, "God, this is shitty food."

Figuratively speaking

"Literally" speaking! "It's literally raining cats and dogs," exclaims a local weatherman.

Final Solution

No such thing, thank God.

First-rate

Third-rate at Walmart if you're lucky!

Flower power

What happened to "The Revolution?"

Foregone conclusion

Utter these words about this or that situation, and I guarantee you'll reach the wrong conclusion.

Fortress America

"Once upon a time, in a galaxy far, far away. . . ."

৵৽

FOX News Brainroom

Home alone.

৵৽

Free money

No kidding—this is what millions of Americans actually believe Barack Obama's 2009 stimulus package consists of. Stay tuned for the presentation of the bill.

৵৽

Free spirit

99% of the time, a person dragging the ball-and-chain of an egregiously erroneous self-appraisal. Show me someone who boasts that he or she is a free spirit and I'll show you a loser.

⊱⊰

Free trade

Don't tell it to my rancher father-in-law.

⊱⊰

Free will

Ambrose Bierce: Free will, O mortals, is a dream: Ye all are chips upon a stream.

⊱⊰

French vodka

"What about Gray Goose?" you ask. Sorry. Even C+ Polish vodkas make the overrated GG taste like dishwater.

ॐ

Friendly competition

Just win, baby!

ॐ

Friendly persuasion

Don't tell it to a Sicilian godfather.

ॐ

Full confession

In the confessional, in the interrogation room, and especially in public, we never fully confess, least of all to ourselves.

Gentleman's agreement

Get it in writing, guys and gals; and even then. . . .

Gentleman's gentleman

A snitch in the service of a cad.

Golden years

My wife's 70-year-old grandmother, survivor of breast can-
cer late in life: "The golden years aren't so golden."

ఇ∙ઓ

Good Friday

Enough said.

ఇ∙ઓ

Good times

A distant American memory: ca. 2009.

ఇ∙ઓ

Grading standards

Check out the website www.pickaprof.com.

ॐ≫

Granny knot

Not a knot for long.

ॐ≫

Great Helmsman

Mao Zedong, who sank China's opportunity to become a civilized nation after he took power in 1949: along with Stalin and Hitler, the most notorious butcher of the twentieth century.

ॐ≫

Gun control

Tell it to the kids at Columbine and Virginia Tech.

Gunboat diplomacy

Walking softly and shaking a big stick.

Habeas Corpus

The dictionary defines HC as "One of a variety of writs that may be issued to bring a party before a court or judge, having as its function the release of the party from unlawful restraint." "Unlawful restraint" = an oxymoron in itself, especially under the George W. Bush administration.

Halcyon days

See "Good times."

᭩᭭

Half-baked

More often than not, this charitable phrase really means not baked at all.

᭩᭭

Heartfelt apology

Apology.

᭩᭭

Hell's Angels

QED!

Helpmate

This one-word oxymoron refers to husbands 100% of the time.

Hemingway hero

Not a hero; not even resembling Hemingway, though Hemingway would've claimed otherwise before punching you in the nose.

Highbrow

Once upon a time in America and Britain, this word wasn't necessarily oxymoronic, but no more. See "Masterpiece Theater."

Hobson's choice

In the culture of baseball, this oxymoron is a toss-up between my poor San Francisco Giants and the Chicago Cubs, as the two most pathetic baseball franchises of the last fifty years. The once-derided New York Mets at least have won two World Series during that time.

Hollywood actor

Let's see: Kevin Costner? Tom Cruise? Bruce Willis? Clint Eastwood? Guess not.

Home schooling

Would you perform surgery on your own kids?

Humble pie

A rare delicacy, said by some to be invented by the French: a doubtful proposition.

Hunky-dory

A-OK in your dreams!

Hush-hush operation

A military plan kept secret until someone opens his mouth, which he always does.

Iberia's pilot

Robert Hendrickson, in his excellent compendium *The Facts on File: Encyclopedia of Word and Phrase Origins*, identifies this as a little-known laudatory nickname of Columbus, the "great navigator" who imagined that he knew where he was not.

Ideation session

The Sink of Bethesda of corporate creativity.

Inadmissible evidence

Evidence.

In-depth

Not on FOX and CNN, which feature shallow-end news anchors like Shepard Smith and Robin Meade.

Innocuous desuetude

Hendrickson identifies this highfalutin term as referring to the former status of a law—seemingly harmlessly dormant for years, only to pop up again at precisely the wrong moment; of course!

"Instant classic"

Only on contemporary American pop music stations! What happened to the past?

Intellectual elite

Most intellectuals I knew in the university were far from being elite, though many of them were elitist.

Intelligence or IQ test

All such tests really do is test the subject's ability to perform on such tests; not a very smart way to measure human intelligence.

Intelligent Design

Design.

Intelligent life in the universe

OK, a bit of a stretch.

Ironic coincidence

In some instances, a coincidence may indeed be ironic; but when an ESPN reporter begins a sentence with "Ironically," as in, "Ironically, A shares the same birth date, the same birth place, and the same middle name with B," he's talking about coincidence, not irony. Something ironic is "contrary to what was expected or intended."

Jerusalem cherry

A Brazilian plant that has nothing to do with the Holy City, nor is it remotely related to cherry trees: a clear instance of botanical wishful thinking.

Job's comforters

Anyone familiar with the Book of Job knows what lies behind this oxymoron. Beyond cold, the "comfort" extended to Job by his three meddlesome friends was downright frigid.

Just deserts

Poetic justice: a pernicious myth, as Shakespeare's innocent Cordelia would've been the first to tell you.

Kentucky colonel

"Kentucky colonel": a patently oxymoronic title having little to do with the state of Kentucky and nothing to do with military rank. KFC, now that's something else.

ॐॐ

Knowledge management

QED!

ॐॐ

Last laugh

No mortal in this vale of soul-making has the last laugh. "Are you laughing at me, Lord?" Thomas Becket asked, shortly before being murdered in his own cathedral in 1187.

ॐॐ

Last word

In the film "Mommy Dearest," when they learn their mother has cut them out of her will, Joan Crawford's son tells his sister,
"Well, mother had the last word, as usual."
Planning to write the scathing memoir *Mommy Dearest*, the daughter asks rhetorically, "Did she?" See "Last laugh."

Latin lover

Ask an Italian wife.

Laughing Philosopher

Hendrickson identifies this as a nickname given to a fifth-century Greek thinker named Democritus. Clearly one of a kind! Philosophy is no laughing matter, as Jean-Paul Sartre would've been the first to tell you.

Lead-pipe cinch

If, as Hendrickson claims, the "lead pipe" in question may be a blackjack, then "lead-pipe cinch" is no oxymoron. Otherwise. . . .

⤞⤝

Learning experience

Experience.

⤞⤝

Learning facilitator

LF: an educational *apparatchik* specializing in getting in the way.

⤞⤝

Leisure industry

Sounds oxymoronic, anyway . . .

Leisure Studies

One of those *faux* college majors, along with General Studies and Family Studies, made up expressly for American athletes. In this case, lots of leisure, little academic work, for jocks. Not to be confused with Hotel Management, a major which actually requires something of students.

Leonine contract

Hendrickson convincingly traces this phrase to an Aesop's fable in which a lion signs on to hunt with a group of other beasts, as long as he keeps all the spoils for himself.

Lesson plans

Ask a creative teacher: Any resemblance between the lesson plan (made up to keep the curriculum coordinator and the principal at bay) and what goes on in the classroom is purely coincidental. This is as it should be.

Lifetime warranty

The Hubble Space Telescope being out of reach, don't bother trying to read the fine print.

Lingua franca

A rickety Babel of miscommunication and obscurity: Pidgin English, for instance; so-named, I suspect, because it reminds one of the babbling of pigeons. Spend three years in Hawaii and you'll know what I mean.

Loganberry

See "Blueberry."

Logical conclusion

Logical according to the strict rules of logic and little else; for "little else," read common sense.

Long green

Not in this shortfall economy, gentlemen.

Los Angeles

That this insane suburb of Purgatory—America's capital of crime, pollution, and hellish traffic—loosely translates as "City of the Angels," makes it the ultimate oxymoron.

Lovable losers

The Cubs, you say? Wait till they win a World Series, then start losing all over again.

Love child

"Lust child" makes better sense.

Love money

Hendrickson traces this phrase to the custom of lovers breaking coins in two, each keeping a half as a guarantee of fidelity forever. You get what you pay for.

ॐॐ

Love nest

See "Love child."

ॐॐ

Loyal opposition

Loyal, that is, until he or she comes out on the short end.

ॐॐ

Luck of the Irish

Tell it to Charles Stewart Parnell, Michael Collins, and Bobby Sands.

Maginot Line

"Invincible" military barrier, or: hot butter to the knife of Germany's thrust into France during WW II.

Man of letters

Once upon a time "man of letters" wasn't an oxymoron, but as we speak it's a sad and sorry archaism.

Managed burn

Tell it to Yellowstone National Park during the fire season of 1988, when the Forest Service let virtually every tree in the park burn to the ground.

Manifest Destiny

The Big Lie of the nineteenth century: neither manifest nor destiny.

Martian canals

Don't tell it to Percival Lowell or Ray Bradbury.

Marxist theory

A cruel and unusual series of economic, social, and political propositions having no solid basis in theory, much less in reality, as Leon Trotsky would've been the first to tell you.

"Masterpiece Theater"

In truth, the "M" in MT ought to stand for "Middlebrow." For the most part this insufferably stuffy and tedious British institution is neither a venue for masterpieces nor, strictly speaking, a theater.

Mature audiences

Why are "M" ratings typically directed at audiences with an ontological age of fifteen?

Meat and potatoes

"Don't get your meat where you get your potatoes."

ஐஷ

Method acting

"Just be yourself." That's acting?

ஐஷ

Money talks

It hardly whispers these days, ca. 2009. "Croaks" is a better word.

ஐஷ

Montessori Method

Letting kids run amok in the classroom as a premise for educating them? Excuse me? "Method" seems the wrong word. Maria, of course, would disagree. See "Method acting."

જ્જ

Moral victory

Defeat.

જ્જ

Mutual non-aggression pact

Ask Uncle Joe Stalin how he felt about *that* when Hitler invaded the Soviet Union in 1941.

જ્જ

Natural aristocracy

In nature!

⤫

Necessary evil

No evil is necessary, damn it.

⤫

Negative capability

Few of us exercise what John Keats called negative capability, or the capability not to "go there"—especially if to do so is ill-advised.

⤫

Neighborhood cooperative

See how many show up for the "Hole Digging Party" to build the neighborhood sign.

Non-judgmental

My wife recently served on a jury in Pima County, Arizona. Interviewing the jury pool, the judge asked an Oriental lady if there was any reason she couldn't reach an objective judgment in the case. "I'm Buddhist, your Honor," she explained. "We are forbidden to judge." She was picked for the jury anyway! At the end of the trial, the jury voted 8-1 for acquittal.[2] Guess who cast the one vote against.

---

2. A civil case in Superior Court, this wrongful death lawsuit required only nine jurors, with seven votes necessary for guilt or acquittal.

Norwegian delicacy

Avoid jellied cod in brine as you would enemy air space.

Nothing wrong

Oliver Wendell Holmes, Jr. (1841-1935), the great American jurist and legal historian, didn't speak until he was almost five years old. Needless to say, his parents were frantic, but no one knew what to do. Then, at the dinner table one Sunday, after the first course was served the boy pushed his chair back.

"The soup's cold," he said.

It was his astonished parents' turn to be mute. Finally the father exclaimed,

"Why didn't you say something before?"

"Nothing was wrong before," the son replied.

Objective criterion

QED!

Official explanation

"Obfuscation" is clearer.

Online learning

To true learning what phone sex is to sex.

Open mind

As an oxymoron, "open mind" is pretty much—as my brother the Superior Court judge would say—a "zipper": an open and shut case.

Opposites attract

No, they don't, damn it. Husbands and wives with nothing in common go opposite ways ASAP.

Orderly bankruptcy

Orderly or disorderly, what does it matter?

Pacification Program

During the Vietnam War, a military operation which resulted in turning the South Vietnamese civilian population—that we were supposed to protect—against us.

Paradise, California

Paradise, CA: hilly community featuring run-down housing and double-wide mobile homes up on jacks; where aging hippies go to smoke dope and die. See "Carefree, Arizona."

Parkway

I still love George Carlin's line, "Why do we park on a driveway and drive on a parkway?"

Peace with honor

Tell that to Richard Nixon and Henry Kissinger.

Permanent

Why do they call women's hairdos "perms" when they last three months tops?

Pole dancing

No kidding: as of April 2009, pole "dancing" is seriously being touted as a future Olympic event. Stay tuned.

Pravda

All the news not fit to print; a tissue of lies. (Pravda means "truth" in Russian).

Pro bono

Remember what paves the road to hell.

❧

"Qualified minority"

Don't get me wrong; I'm certainly not saying that minorities are *ipso facto* unqualified for positions. As an oxymoron, however, the phrase "qualified minority" is a staple of job descriptions of affirmative-action-driven employers, especially in academe, where I plied my trade for nearly forty years. Administrators love it because it lets them have their cake and eat it too. Two things are lost in the shuffle: to be "qualified" for a job doesn't mean that you're the most worthy applicant, *all* of whom are qualified—i.e., have doctoral degrees, say.

More pernicious still, although they won't admit it, administrators under the gun of affirmative action sanctions know that they need a certain quota of minority hires, the more the merrier. In other words, and in the heyday of affirmative action in the eighties and nineties and beyond, all a minority needed to "qualify" for the job was a warm body and the willingness to show up for class most of the time. Again, this isn't a rap on minorities; it's a slap, rather, at duplicitous administrators who say they're doing one thing while doing another.

❧

Queen's taste

Hendrickson identifies this phrase as American, not British. Good thing, because the 83-year-old Queen Elizabeth II, bless her heart, continues to wear those atrocious hats.

Rap music

Enough said, except that the rap against rap music is richly deserved.

Reality programming

Contemporary TV offerings: as tedious and stupid as they are highly orchestrated and edited.

Received idea

See "Conventional wisdom."

Redemptive suffering

Only for those redeemed by not having to suffer.

Red-letter days

Color them blue in this economy, ca. 2009.

Restraining order

Tell that to battered wives and girlfriends.

<hr />

Robust incoherence

See the comic strip "Doonesbury," 10/24/09.

<hr />

Roman peace

See "Carthaginian peace."

<hr />

Rush hour

Standing still in traffic for sixty minutes constitutes a "rush?" I don't think so. See "Los Angeles."

Sacred cow

Nothing is sacred, certainly not in America's debased culture of entertainment. *Cf.* the execrable "American Idol" and its spin-offs.

Safe sex

We're not talking epidemiology here! See "Love child."

Sanitary landfill

Don't you love it?

કેન્ઙ

Scheduled arrival

See "Scheduled Departure."

કેન્ઙ

Scheduled departure

"Be sure to get to the airport early." Right—so that your wait won't exceed more than three-and-a-half hours.

કેન્ઙ

Security Council resolution

. . . Or what the tyrannical king in the *Wizard of Id* comic strip laughingly calls "a hoot."

Self-esteem

Ambrose Bierce: "An erroneous appraisement."

Self-knowledge

An animal thought to be extinct: certainly an antonym of self-esteem. See "Self-esteem."

Sensitivity training

Add the prefix "In-" to "sensitivity," and the oxymoron vanishes.

తోన్⁶

Serial killer

"Serial killer" is a *psychological* oxymoron. As many shrinks have argued, murder usually involves a projection of the self onto the other. That is, in the dark recesses of the psyche until he runs out of targets or runs out of time, the serial killer keeps killing one person over and over: himself. Only then, unless prevented from doing so, does he put a gun to his head. Every murder, as Jung put it, is a suicide in disguise.

తోన్⁶

Shavian wit

As a playwright, George Bernard Shaw was pretty good; as a wit, he was much overrated. His famous "Those who can, do; those who can't, teach," is a crock. Teaching IS doing.

తోన్⁶

Slick Willie

President Bill Clinton, who got caught with a cigar; at least no one accused him of inhaling *that* time around.

Society Islands

No one lives in the Society Islands.

Sotto voce

Not at the Monday morning Ladies' Coffee Club in Swan Lake, Montana!

Standard Operating Procedure

A SOP thrown to SNAFU!

છે—

Stanislavski Method

See "Method acting." See "Montessori Method."

છે—

Street justice

Cops know, or should know, what this means.

છે—

Sub Rosa

Fat chance!

Suzerain fealty

This medieval system of supposed loyalties extended from the vassal to the lord and even the King. In reality it was punctuated by betrayals and desertions, especially on the part of vassals, who were prone to disappear into the woods when the king's men came looking for recruits to join a crusade to the Holy Land.

Sweet nuptials

Until the honeymoon ends . . . and sometimes until it begins.

Sweet science

Middleweight fighter Michael Nunn: "I wouldn't wish this profession on my worst enemy."

കൈ

Sweetness and Light

Neither nor.

കൈ

Teachable moment

Moment.

കൈ

Thousand-year Reich

Only twelve miserable years, thank God![3]

ॐ

Thumbs up

When the ridiculously generous film critics Siskel and Roper give a film "Two thumbs up," you can usually count on the opposite.

ॐ

Time flies

Time doesn't come and go too fast; *we* do.

ॐ

———————

3. I consider the beginning of the Third Reich as 1933, the year Hitler was appointed Chancellor of Germany.

Tit for tat

The psychology of revenge being what it is, this neat expression should actually read "Tit for tat for tit for. . . ." ad infinitum. Read *Hamlet* if you don't believe this.

Tone it down

"Tone it up" at the Monday morning Ladies' Coffee Club in Swan Lake, Montana.

Top shelf

In bars and taverns, what usually passes for "top-shelf" booze is really just a cut above bottom shelf, or well liquor. Anyone who thinks Stoli or Absolut is top-shelf ought to try Polish Polonaise or "bison grass" vodka.

Top-drawer

See "Top-shelf."

Transcendent vacuity

See the comic strip "Doonesbury," 10/24/09.

Treasure State

Montana: alas, no gold, silver or sapphires worth mentioning in the 21st century.

Tricky Dick

"Tricky," that is, until the so-called eighteen-minute gap. See "Slick Willie."

৶৽৻

Trojans

This is the nickname of the "mighty men of Troy" (University of Southern California), who forget that the Trojans had their butts kicked by the Greeks.

৶৽৻

True fact

A wonderful phrase coined by one of my freshman concerning something neither true nor factual.

৶৽৻

Ugly as sin

If sins were ugly, who would be tempted by them? Would you have bitten into a wormy apple in the Garden?

Under your hat

See "Hush-hush operation."

United Nations

See "Security Council Resolution."

Unlimited potential

Catch-phrase for losers; commonly on the lips of doting mothers who have to say something.

 споро

Unlimited warranty

See "Lifetime warranty."

 споро

Unwilling participant

All participants are willing, whether they wish to be or not.

 споро

Utah!

(. . . As seen on the official state license plate).

   This sorry state and the exclamation point are at definite loggerheads. No one ever thought to write a dynamic Broadway musical featuring the residents of Orderville, Standardville, Centerville, Circleville, or Virgin.

Vendetta

See "Tit for tat."

Vermont charity

Hendrickson quotes Hugh Rawlins in *Wicked Words* (1989): ". . . [Vermont charity is] a symbol of cheapness, or what hoboes call 'sympathy which is accompanied by little else.'"

Wasted pitch

The second-best[4] Satchel Paige anecdote I know was told to me by my friend John Dorn from Mankato, Minnesota, where his dad played semi-pro baseball in the 30's. One day the Kansas City Monarchs, a touring Negro team, came to town: on the mound, Satchel Paige. Paige threw John's dad two high heaters, which he swung at futilely. I asked John if, in an 0-2 situation, Paige decided to waste one—as most pitchers would—to see if the batter would go for it. (Of course John's dad's team was hopelessly outclassed by the Monarchs, several of whom, including Paige, should've played in the majors.)

Not a chance. Wasting no time and showing no mercy, Paige threw a blinding fastball down the pipe; John's dad struck out with the lumber on his shoulder.

4. The best story was told by a journalist who saw Paige pitch in his prime. Sitting on the third base side and up a few rows, he had a perfect side view of Paige's deliveries to the plate. Paige had a wonderful repertory of pitches, of course, but every time he threw a fastball, the journalist swore up and down that he *couldn't see it* after it left Paige's hand and before it thumped the catcher's glove.

White lie

A lie is a lie is a lie.

꿍

Workers' paradise

Tell it to the Russians 1917-1989.

꿍

About the Author

In 2005 Steven Carter retired as Emeritus Professor of English after teaching in the university for thirty-eight years. The author of fourteen books published here and abroad, he served as Senior Fulbright Fellow at two Polish universities in 1991. He is the only two-time winner of Italy's coveted *Nuove Lettere* International Poetry and Literature Prize. Carter and his wife Janice divide the year between Arizona and Montana.

www.ingramcontent.com/pod-product-compliance
Lightning Source LLC
Chambersburg PA
CBHW031630130726
47900CB00018B/741